Submarines – More Than Tasty Sandwiches

There are some basic problems with staying underneath the water for any length of time. One problem is breathing, since a person needs air to stay alive. Another problem is water pressure – the weight of the water on a person's body. If you have ever picked up a gallon of water, you have felt its weight in your hands. Now imagine thousands of gallons of water over your head. You can see how quickly the pressure becomes unbearable as a person dives deeper.

Some of the first underwater divers used diving bells. These were made of thick, heavy metal or weighted barrels. A large bell was placed directly over the water and then lowered straight down until the bottom was reached. A small bell was placed on a person's head and then tied down securely. The top part of the bell remained filled with air. Early divers could not do much with these crude tools. They also had a very short time before their air supply was out and they needed to be lifted to the surface.

The idea of the undersea boat goes far back into history. With such a vessel, people could not only stay under the water, but they could move around to different locations.

Around 1620, a Dutch scientist named Cornelius van Drebbel showed his idea of an undersea rowboat in England. The design was covered in waterproof hides. Since then, other men have invented different types of undersea boats, and by World War I submarines were being used to sink battleships.

On the surface, a modern submarine works very much like other large boats – but submarines spend very little time above water. The submarine is designed with an outer hull that is pressure proof. This keeps the crew and equipment from being crushed as the vessel dives deeper into the water. Also, tanks inside the hull fill with water to give the submarine ballast, or weight.

Once under the surface, the submarine has other special tools for getting around. An engine powers the propellers that drive the vessel and rudders help to steer it. Steel fins, called diving planes, help with diving, and a periscope can be used to see long distances (much like a telescope). A sail that is 20 feet high rises from the ship's deck and holds the periscope and radio equipment in place.

The modern submarine can stay underwater for months at a time. Some submarines have traveled underneath the ice at the North Pole and others all the way around the globe underwater.

So, the next time you eat a submarine sandwich, you might think about the amazing undersea vessel that it is named after.

Write the answers.

1. What was the diving bell made of?

_____

_____

2. Name two problems with staying underwater for a long time.

_____and_____

3. When was the first undersea rowboat design shown in England?

_____

4. How was the submarine used in World War I?

_____

5. Why is the outer hull important to a submarine?

_____

_____

6. What makes the submarine able to dive, and how does it work?

_____

_____

_____

7. Name three special tools that help the submarine get around.

_____

_____

8. How long can a modern submarine stay underwater?

_____

Draw a line from each word to the meaning used in the story.

securely   • used for steering

crude   • tightly

rudder   • simple

ballast   • engine-powered blades
                              for moving forward

periscope   • weight

hide   • used for seeing long
                              distances

propeller   • outer covering

hull   • animal skin

Design and draw your own submarine. Include the sail, propellers, and rudder.

Rings Around the Planet

While our home is the third planet from the sun, our neighbor, Saturn, is the sixth. It is second in size to Jupiter, which is the largest planet in the solar system.

Saturn is best known for its ring system and is mostly made of hydrogen gas. Toward the center of the planet, the hydrogen gas condenses into a liquid. Even closer to the center, the liquid hydrogen is compressed into metallic hydrogen. And finally at the center, there is thought to be a small, rocky core with a temperature near to 27,000° F. Now that's super hot!

Scientists have determined that a full rotation of the planet (one Saturn day) takes about 10 and a half hours. That's more than twice as fast as Earth's 24-hour rotation. Though the days may be much shorter than ours, it takes 29.6 Earth years for Saturn to make a complete orbit around the sun. That's about 10,804 days instead of 365 for Earth's smaller orbit.

Saturn's Rings

The rings of Saturn were first seen by Italian scientist Galileo in 1610. He was using one of the very first telescopes, so he thought that the rings were more like handles.

With better telescopes, the rings were later found to be separate from the planet and were labeled "A" through "E". Each ring is thought to consist of collections of rock, frozen gases, and ice. These objects can be as small as dust particles or as big as boulders.

Saturn's Moons

Saturn has 18 known moons. The planet may also have 14 new moons that have not been studied.

Most of Saturn's moons consist primarily of light, icy materials. Each moon has a name and a history of its own. Some are covered in craters and others are smoother.

Phoebe is the farthest moon from Saturn. It orbits in the opposite direction of the planet's other moons. Scientists suspect that Phoebe is probably a comet or part of one captured by Saturn's gravitational field.

Titan is the largest of Saturn's moons. Scientists believe it is larger than the planet Mercury. However, the exact size of Titan is not known because of a thick orange haze that hides its surface.

Visitors From Earth

The United States has sent many mechanical visitors into space. The Pioneer 11 probe flew by Saturn in 1979 and was followed by Voyager 1 in 1980 and Voyager 2 in 1981.

More recently, the National Aeronautics and Space Administration (NASA) sent the Cassini spacecraft toward Saturn in 1997. This spacecraft reached Saturn in 2004.

Cassini is designed to study Saturn and its moons. It even launched a probe, called the Huygens, into the atmosphere of the moon Titan. With Cassini, scientists are hoping to get better pictures and information about Saturn, its rings, and especially Titan.

Rings Around the Planet

Fill in the circle to finish the sentences.

1. Next to Jupiter, Saturn is the _____.

   ○ smallest planet in the solar system
   ○ roundest planet in the solar system
   ○ largest planet in the solar system

2. Saturn is mostly made of _____.

   ○ carbon dioxide gas
   ○ oxygen gas
   ○ hydrogen gas

3. One Saturn day equals _____.

   ○ $10\frac{1}{2}$ hours
   ○ 24 hours
   ○ 29 hours

4. Saturn has _____ known moons.

   ○ 14
   ○ 18
   ○ 2

5. The rings of Saturn are thought to consist of _____.

   ○ rocks, dust, and light
   ○ rocks, frozen gases, and ice
   ○ lava, frozen gases, and ice

6. In 2004, the _____.

   ○ Voyager spacecraft returned from Saturn
   ○ Cassini spacecraft arrived at Titan
   ○ Cassini spacecraft arrived at Saturn

Rings Around the Planet

Mark an X to show which planet is being described.

About the Planet	Saturn	Earth
I am the sixth planet from the sun.		
I have 18 known moons.		
I am the third planet from the sun.		
I have a $10\frac{1}{2}$ hour day.		
There are 365 days in my year.		
My moon does not have a thick orange haze.		
My core is small, hard, and rocky.		
One of my moons is larger than the planet Mercury.		
I am surrounded by rings.		
My NASA probes have been sent to visit far away places.		

Pretend you are a space probe collecting information.
Write some things you know about planet Earth.

_____

_____

Timber Wolves

The timber wolf is a member of the gray wolf species within the dog family. Although it looks a lot like a German shepherd dog, it is bigger. The wolf's snout and legs are longer than a dog's.

The color of a wolf can vary, but it is usually gray. Most adult male wolves weigh between 75 and 120 pounds (34 to 54 kilograms). They have 42 teeth, including four fangs at the front of their mouths. These fangs can be up to two inches long.

The warm, bushy fur of a timber wolf allows its body to withstand cold climates, and its feet are large to help it walk on snow. Many timber wolves live in wooded habitats in northern areas like Alaska and Canada. There are also small numbers of wolves found in Minnesota, Michigan, Wisconsin, Montana, Idaho, and Washington.

Living in groups, or packs, of 8 to 20, wolves are believed to have very strong feelings for each other. They also have a very clear social or ranking order within the pack. There are dominant members (the leaders) and subordinate members (the followers). All must follow strict rules for showing respect or rank.

The dominant male and female control where the pack stays, when it hunts, and how it raises the pups. When pack members meet, the dominant member stands up tall while the subordinate members crouch down. Once again, this is an indication of rank.

Each wolf pack lives in an area called a territory, which can cover between 30 and 800 square miles. Often attacking outsiders, the pack does not allow other wolves to hunt in its territory.

With superb eyesight, hearing, and sense of smell, the clever-minded wolf is an excellent hunter. The hunt begins with howling, which can get very loud as a way of warning outsider wolves to stay away.

Since many of the animals they hunt are bigger and faster, like caribou and elk, wolves have to be quick, too. Wolves will eat almost any animal they can catch, working as a team to finish the job.

Throughout history people have feared the wolf, even though they are known to keep away from people. They were often shown as the evil character in stories. They were thought to be a threat to farmers because they could kill sheep and cattle. And their ghostly sounding howls added to the fear.

In some areas of the world, wolves have been wiped out completely. However, in the United States, timber wolves have been reintroduced into the wild in Wyoming and Idaho, where they once roamed in great numbers.

Write the answers.

1. What type of habitat do timber wolves like?

_____

_____

2. What animal is the timber wolf compared to in the story.

_____

3. Write three things that you learned about a wolf pack.

_____

4. Why do wolves howl?

_____

5. Why are wolves excellent hunters?

_____

_____

6. Why do you think people have feared wolves in the past?

_____

_____

_____

Write the correct description for each category.

Timber Wolf
Hair (color and type):
Weight/size:
Similar looking animals:
Foot size: ___small   ___medium   ___large
Teeth:
Home state(s):
Other interesting facts:

You may have read or heard stories where the wolf
is the bad or evil character. List a few of these stories below.

_____

_____

_____

_____

Let's Learn About Speleology

Speleology can be described as the study of cavities large enough for a person to stand in. So do speleologists study rotten dinosaur teeth? No. They study caves.

Any natural hollow space that is big enough to enter is considered a cave. Some caves end within a few steps, while others can stretch on for miles with many interconnecting passageways. The largest cave ever explored is the Mammoth-Flint Ridge Cave in Kentucky. This cave goes on for 340 miles, and scientists believe there is even more of it to be discovered.

Caves are formed in different ways. Some caves are formed over thousands of years as underground water wears away rock. Within that time, the earth may shift or the surroundings may change so the rock is exposed and most of the water drained away. What remains is known as a solution cave.

A lava tube cave is formed from hot flowing lava. What happens is the outer lava cools and hardens while the hot lava inside continues to flow. The hot lava finally drains from the tube to create a cave.

The third type of cave is a sea cave. These are formed from ocean waters as they erode the rocky shoreline.

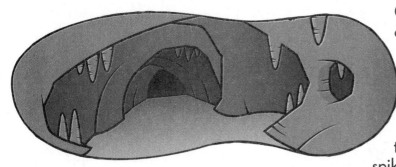

Caves are usually dark, damp, and covered with strange formations called speleothems. Most of the eerie looking speleothems are made by trickling or seeping water. Of these formations, stalactites are the icicle-shaped spikes hanging down from the ceiling and stalagmites are the spikes that rise from the floor of the cave, or ground. A stalactite and a stalagmite can meet to form a column.

If you have trouble keeping stalactites and stalagmites straight, just remember that the one with the "g" (stalagmite) forms on the ground.

Even though they are dark and damp, caves have always been a good shelter for people. In some caves, prehistoric people drew artwork on the walls. These cave pictures show images of how they lived and survived in the times before written language and machinery.

Animals have also found shelter in caves. Bats are known to roost in caves during the day, flying out at night in large groups to hunt for insects. Other animals living in caves can include birds, rats, raccoons, and insects. And some bears use caves for a winter den.

But only very specialized animals called troglobites can live in the deepest, darkest part of caves where there is no light or wind. Such animals include certain fish, beetles, and spiders. Most troglobites are blind and have a thin or colorless skin or shell. They all have an excellent sense of smell and touch to make up for their lack of sight.

Hobbie Facts: If someone asks you to go spelunking, be sure to grab a helmet, a flashlight, some warm clothing, a pair of sturdy shoes, and some climbing gear because you are going cave exploring!

Write the answers.

1. How big does a hole have to be in order to be considered a true cave?

_____

2. Where is the largest cave ever explored?

_____

3. What are three animals that live in caves?

_____

4. What is it like inside a cave? How does it look and feel?

_____

5. Describe how a lava tube cave is formed.

_____

_____

6. What are two types of speleothems?

_____

7. Where do troglobites live?

_____

8. List four things that you would need to go spelunking.

_____

_____

_____

Describe and draw three things you learned about caves from the story

_____

_____

_____

_____

_____

_____

_____

_____

_____

The story tells about the things needed for spelunking. Write the name of your favorite hobby and list four things you need to do it.

Your Hobby: _____

_____

_____

A complete simple sentence tells one complete thought.
A compound sentence contains two or more complete simple sentences or thoughts, often joined by a conjunction such as **and**, **but**, or **or**.

Complete simple sentences: Snow skiing is fun.
You must be careful while you ski.

Compound sentence: Snow skiing is fun, but you must be careful while you ski.

Read each sentence. Write **S** if it is simple or **C** if it is compound.

1. My family and I go skiing each winter in Colorado. _____

2. My brother likes to snowboard, but dad likes to use two skis. _____

3. My sister Jean will try skiing again this time. _____

4. She wants to ride the lift up on her own this year. _____

5. Last year she tried to ride the lift, but she was too frightened. _____

6. My mother had to help her off, and Jean was embarrassed. _____

Combine the two simple sentences to make a compound sentence using **and**, **but**, or **or**.

7. My family shopped for skiing supplies. We all didn't find what we needed.

_____

_____

8. My brother found the gloves he liked. He found the suit he wanted.

_____

_____

9. The suit was bright red. It had racing stripes.

_____

_____

10. My brother thought he might buy it. He could use his old suit another year.

_____

_____

No Run-Ons Allowed!

A **run-on sentence** contains two or more sentences that have been incorrectly joined. Usually a run-on sentence has incorrect punctuation or no conjunction.

Run–on sentence: Baseball is played in the summer football is enjoyed in the fall.
Corrected punctuation: Baseball is played in the summer. Football is enjoyed in the fall.
Use of conjunction: Baseball is played in the summer, but football is enjoyed in the fall.

Read each sentence. If it is a run-on sentence, write **RO**. If the sentence is correct, write **C**.

1. In the summer, there are concerts in the park we like to take a picnic with us. _____

2. I took my friend to a concert. We had a wonderful time. _____

3. One concert was so crowded that we couldn't find a place to sit. _____

4. The park is always crowded many people come to the concerts. _____

5. The band continues to play after dark I bring a flashlight with me. _____

Rewrite each run-on sentence as two separate sentences.

6. My friend Amanda went to every concert sometimes we would meet at the park and sit together.

_____

_____

7. Every Monday a different band would play for the eager crowd we heard a variety of music.

_____

_____

8. My family really enjoyed the jazz band the best they brought my father up on stage.

_____

_____

Correct the run on sentences below by adding **and**, **but**, or **or**.

9. I will always remember the summer concerts ∧ the fun we had
   (and)

10. My father said he was embarrassed to go on stage he had a good time.

11. Dad likes playing the piano he likes playing the saxophone.

12. These are wonderful summer memories I will never forget them.

Positively Possessive Nouns

A possessive noun is a noun that shows ownership.
Look at the guidelines on how to write nouns in possessive form.

singular noun	add **'s**	boy's dog
plural noun ending in **s**	add **'**	girls' dresses
plural noun not ending in **s**	add **'s**	men's suits

Read each sentence. Write **S** or **P** above each underlined possessive noun to identify it as singular or plural.

1. <u>Marla's</u> friend, Katlyn, likes to go to the pet shop with her every Monday

2. The girls became interested in rabbits at the <u>store's</u> grand opening.

3. The <u>friends'</u> mothers took them to the opening.

4. The <u>store's</u> owner was pleased to have so many people attend.

5. Marla and Katlyn rushed to the <u>rabbits'</u> hutches.

6. The young <u>ladies'</u> mothers bought each a rabbit.

7. <u>Fluffy's</u> hutch was designed and built by <u>Katlyn's</u> neighbor.

8. <u>Marla's</u> rabbit lives in her back yard with complete freedom.

Write the possessive form of each noun.

9. rabbit	_____	dog	_____
10. pet store	_____	friend	_____
11. mayor	_____	veterinarian	_____
12. geese	_____	neighbors	_____
13. canaries	_____	women	_____
14. girls	_____	windows	_____

Subject pronouns can take the place of a noun that is the subject of the sentence. These are the only pronouns that can be used as the subject of the sentence.

__Singular__	__Plural__
I	we
you	you
he, she, it	they

Underline the **subject pronoun** in each sentence.

1. I once sang with a group for the school talent show.

2. It was a wonderful song about springtime.

3. We rehearsed several times before the big night.

4. You would have enjoyed the show.

5. It had everything from magic acts to song and dance routines.

Write a **subject pronoun** that can replace the subject in each sentence.

6. Kathy and Tom performed a jazz routine. _____

7. Kathy was nervous, but calmed down once they started. _____

8. Tom was excited to get the routine over with. _____

9. Rebecca and Katy each played beautiful piano solos. _____

10. Katy had practiced for weeks to memorize her solo. _____

11. Katy, Rebecca, and I felt it was the best show ever. _____

12. Yesterday, Steven gave Katy an article from the paper. _____

13. The newspaper had a picture of her performing her talent. _____

Oh! Those Object Pronouns

Object pronouns can take the place of nouns. They follow action verbs in a sentence or the words **as**, **to**, **with**, **for**, and **at**.

My mother gave <u>Mary and me</u> two warm cookies.

My mother gave <u>us</u> two warm cookies.

Singular	**Plural**
him, her, it	us
you	you
me	them

Write an **object pronoun** that can take the place of the underlines word(s) in each sentence.

1. Steven plays after school with <u>Scott and me</u>. _____

2. Scott throws the baseball at <u>Steven</u>. _____

3. My friend borrowed a book from <u>Abby</u>. _____

4. Abby will return <u>the book</u> tomorrow. _____

5. Annette wrote a story for <u>Mother and me</u>. _____

6. Mother gave <u>Annette</u> a new journal. _____

7. Kendra helped Kevin with <u>his story</u>. _____

8. Kevin likes to play with <u>Kendra and Annette</u>. _____

9. Kathy wanted to play with <u>Kevin and Kendra</u>. _____

Write an **object pronoun** above the underlined word(s).

It was Mrs. Smith's class' turn to arrange for morning announcements. She wanted to come up with something fun and unique for <u>her class</u> to try for announcements. Mrs. Smith had <u>the class</u> write out a script for each day. She told <u>the class</u> to be creative.

James was in charge of the weather. She let <u>James</u> do the weather research for the entire week. He decided he was going to dress as a different character each day. Everyone was surprised he came up the idea. He gave his research to <u>Mrs. Smith</u> to check over before the announcements. After grading his research, she gave <u>James</u> an A for <u>his research</u>.

Tips for using I and me.

Tip #1: Always name yourself last when talking about yourself and another person.
Example: Janice and I   **OR**   Mark and me

Tip #2: When you're not sure whether to use I or me, read the sentence using only I or me.
Example: Sophie and I went to the Library.   **OR**   Sophie and me went to the library.

I went to the library.   **Me** went to the library.

Using the pronoun **I** in this sentence is correct.

- -

Write **I** or **me** to complete each sentence.

1. Several friends and _____ decided to help out with the school paper.

2. Many articles were written by Karen and _____.

3. Mrs. Keller likes the way that Ashley and _____ create advertisements.

4. Bobby and _____ created an advertisement last fall.

5. Mrs. Cundiff and _____ wondered who would take over for Bobby.

6. Mrs. Keller suggested that Karen and _____ work together.

7. Mrs. Cundiff asked if Beth and _____ would like to write an article.

8. We were very excited and _____ couldn't wait to get started.

9. Our article was taken from an interview with the football coach and _____.

10. He had many wonderful things to say about the newspaper and _____.

11. My brother and _____ know coach Randle well.

12. He and _____ had coach Randle for P.E. class.

Challenge: Use a separate sheet of paper to write an essay about a friend or relative and some wonderful adventures you've had together. Use I and me in your sentences. Read your essay to your family or friends and watch them smile!

Amazing Adjectives

An **adjective** is a describing word for nouns and/or pronouns.

Adjectives are the magic of a sentence. They can put life into any sentence or story by adding details and clarity.

> The boys stood on the beach.
> The <u>four</u> <u>young</u> boys stood on the <u>warm</u> <u>sandy</u> beach.

Read each sentence. Underline the **adjectives**.

1. The bright radiant sun was shining on the warm wet backs of the water skiers.

2. My small family was looking forward to taking our shiny new ski boat on the clear lake.

3. It didn't appear that my youngest brother was going to try to use his brand new skis.

4. He wasn't looking forward to the busy wet day ahead of us.

5. My excited parents couldn't wait to introduce my timid brother to water skiing.

Write each word with two **adjectives** to describe it. Circle the noun.

6. lake _____   water _____
7. skier _____   day _____
8. dock _____   ride _____
9. boat _____   swimmer _____

Write your own adjectives to complete the paragraph.

It was a _____ morning for my _____ family. We were looking forward to our _____ trip to the _____ beach. My _____ sister looked for her _____ swimsuit everywhere. My _____ mother had just purchased it at the _____ store, and my _____ sister couldn't wait to wear it. After searching for what seemed like hours, we finally found it. It wasn't in my _____ sister's _____ drawers or in her _____ closet. She had tried it on _____ evening and forgot to take it off.

Celebrating with Verbs

An **action** verb tells what the subject is doing.

My brother <u>ran</u> to the store.

A **linking** verb describes a state being.

My brother <u>was</u> glad the store was open.

Identify the type of verb in each sentence.
Circle **A** if it's an action verb or **L** if it's a linking verb.

1. Janice <u>threw</u> a birthday party for her brother.   A   L

2. She <u>has</u> a thoughtful sister.   A   L

3. Her mother <u>sent</u> the invitations last Thursday.   A   L

4. Janice <u>was</u> glad all the guests could come.   A   L

5. Janice and her friend, Beth, <u>had</u> prepared the party activities.   A   L

6. Her mother <u>was</u> excited everyone was on time.   A   L

Use a **linking** verb and **action** verb to complete the sentences.

had	have	is	was
eaten	enjoying	given	helping	snapping	thanking

7. Robert _____ everyone for coming.

8. Janice_____ the party as much as Robert.

9. His mother _____ pictures of the guests.

10. She _____ Robert the knife to cut the cake.

11. Janice _____ Robert with the cake.

12. The guests _____ every bit of cake

Helpful Verbs

A **helping verb** helps the **main verb** describe the action that happened in the past, is happening in the present, or will happen in the future.

helping verb   main verb

She <u>was</u> <u>reading</u> a wonderful story

Use the helping verbs **am**, **is**, **are**, **was**, or **were** when the main verb ends in **-ing**, or is in present tense.

Use the helping verbs **has**, **have**, or **had** when the main verb end is **-ed**, or is in past tense.

Use the helping verb **will** when the main verb doesn't have a suffix, or is in future tense.

- -

Read each sentence. Circle **HV** if the underlined verb is a helping verb or **MV** if it is a main verb.

1. Jean and I <u>wanted</u> to go to the city library yesterday.   **HV**   **MV**
2. We <u>were</u> looking for some good books to read.   **HV**   **MV**
3. I <u>had</u> asked my mother earlier in the morning.   **HV**   **MV**
4. My mother <u>agreed</u> to drive us to the library.   **HV**   **MV**

- -

Circle the main verb and underline the helping verb in each sentence.

5. The librarian was putting the new books on the shelves.

6. She was listing their titles to us.

7. We were watching her stack the books.

8. Jean and I were hoping to find our favorite ones.

- -

Use the helping verbs am, are, has, have and will to complete the sentences.

9. My mother _____ take us to the library again.

10. She _____ spoken to Jean's mother.

11. They _____ pleased that we like the library.

12. I _____ excited that they have so many good books.

The Amazing Ability of Adverbs

An **adverb** describes a verb. It tells **how**, **when** or **where**.
Most adverbs that tell how end with **-ly**.

Write **how**, **when** or **where** on the line to tell how the adverb would describe a verb.

1. slowly _how_   early _____   then _____   here _____

2. sadly _____   outside _____   later _____   upstairs _____

3. inside _____   never _____   usually _____   rapidly _____

4. off _____   happily _____   there _____   now _____

Circle the adverb in each sentence.

5. Dale and I patiently waited for Mother.

6. She had gone inside the hardware store.

7. Earlier, Mother had read the sale sign.

8. She quickly knew what we needed for our project.

9. We happily worked on our science project.

Underline the verb and circle the adverb in each sentence.
Then circle **how**, **when** or **where** to tell how the adverb describes the verb.

10. I presented my science project (yesterday).   how   (when)   where

11. The entire class completed theirs carefully.   how   when   where

12. We usually hope for good grades.   how   when   where

13. Mrs. Gibson listened attentively to our presentations.   how   when   where

14. We gave the presentations in the lunchroom.   how   when   **where**

Challenge: Pretend you're a sports reporter after a big game.
Write about the game using adverbs. Use a separate piece of paper.

Cooling Off with Good and Well

Good is an adjective to describe a noun.

Lindsey is a **good** swimming instructor.

Well is an adverb used to describe a verb,

She swims **well**.

- -

Circle good or **well** to complete each sentence.

1. Lindsey is (good **well**) at doing the butterfly stroke.

2. She has learned to swim (good **well**).

3. We learned the lesson (good **well**).

4. It is hard to swim (good **well**) in the ocean.

5. The sand feels (good **well**) between my toes.

6. Everyone listens (good **well**) to Lindsey's stories.

7. She showed my sister a (good **well**) way to save others.

8. Lindsey planned her swim schedule (good **well**).

9. It was (good **well**) to see everyone having a good time.

10. She performed (good **well**) at last week's swim meet.

- -

Write good or **well** to complete each sentence.

1. My favorite dessert is ice cream, because it tastes _____.

2. I visited my grandma yesterday and she wasn't feeling _____.

3. We rested _____ at the Beach Front Hotel.

4. I did a _____ job on my science project.

 Challenge: Use construction paper to create a billboard that advertises something. Be sure to use good and well on your billboard.

Preppy Prepositions

A **preposition** shows the connection between other words in a sentence.
A **prepositional phrase** starts with a preposition and ends with a noun or pronoun.

The man was working **beside** the computer.
preposition: beside
prepositional phrase: beside the computer

Use the prepositions in the box to complete each sentence.

Circle the prepositional phrase. Use the list of common prepositions if you need help.

1. The computer is _____ the desk.

2. The windows are _____ the desk.

3. The paper is _____ the books.

4. The chair is _____ the desk.

5. Pens fit _____ the cup.

6. The lamp is _____ the cup of pins.

7. The printer is _____ the desk.

8. The stack _____ papers are nice and neat.

9. No one is _____ the desk.

10. The windows are _____ the computer.

11. The lamp is _____ the edge of the desk.

12. The books _____ the paper are new.

Common Prepositions	
about	above
across	after
along	at
before	behind
below	beside
by	down
during	for
from	in
inside	near
of	off
on	over
under	without

Let the Fireworks Begin!

Helpful Hints to Better Reading Comprehension

- Read the questions first (located on the page after the story).
- Read once for enjoyment and twice for information.
- Underline the title and number of paragraphs.
- Highlight all bold print words.

Let the Fireworks Begin!

One scorching hot summer afternoon, we ventured down Main street to fight the crowd as we watched the parade. It was the Fourth of July! We had waited for this day all year. Not bothered by the heat of the day, we watched the parade that **extended** like a snake down several city blocks. The parade included fire trucks, old cars, and decorated floats from the local stores. It was pretty much the same every year, but we didn't care because it was the parade, and candy was to be thrown from the floats. We knew by the end of the event we'd have bushels and bushels of candy in our possession.

After the parade, my family and I headed back to my uncle's house for a barbecue with my relatives. The first question from my little sister was, "When is the sky going to show us its sparkles?" She believes that fireworks come naturally from above. I hesitated to tell her that fireworks are not born in the sky, but are **launched** with a machine by our local fire department. We waited anxiously as the sun set below the trees. It seemed like it took forever. My sister yelled out every so often, "Isn't it time yet?" She has no patience when it comes to fireworks.

Finally, it was time. As always my parents packed the car with lawn chairs and coolers. We headed out to an empty parking lot to get a closer view. The fireworks began to boom and explode as fast as lightening hitting the sky.

In no time at all, the fireworks show was over and another Fourth of July had passed. It seemed like the day had just started and then was only a memory. I wonder how this fun day got started?

Answer the following questions about "Let the Fireworks Begin!"

Context Clues

1. Write the definition for the word **extended**. Then write a sentence using that word.

_____

_____

2. Write the definition for the word **launched**. Then write a sentence using that word.

_____

_____

3. Number the following sentences in the order they happened in the story.

_____ My family and I headed back for a barbecue.

_____ We had bushels and bushels of candy.

_____ We watched the parade that extended like a snake down several city blocks.

_____ The fireworks show was over and another fourth of July had passed.

_____ Fireworks are launched with a machine by our local fire department.

Drawing Conclusions

4. Describe the younger sister's personality. _____

5. Explain what the older sister meant when she said, "Fireworks are not born in the sky."

_____

6. List specific words or quotes from the story that explain the writer's feelings about this holiday.

_____

Similes

7. Write a simile contained in the story. _____

8. Write a new simile to use in the story. _____

The History of the Fourth of July

Independence Day, also known as the Fourth of July, is a national holiday of the United States of America. Like Christmas, it is a time that families get together. They enjoy barbecue, picnics, and parades.

July 4th, 1776 was the date that the Declaration of Independence was signed by the Continental Congress in Philadelphia. However, Congress did not finally **establish** the Fourth of July as a legal holiday until 1941.

At the time of the signing, the United States consisted of thirteen colonies, under the rule of England's King George III. The public **cry** argued fairness of the thirteen colonies in America being forced to pay taxes to the King of England. The practice was referred to as Taxation Without Representation. The unrest grew in the colonies, so King George sent troops to help control the situation. In 1774, the thirteen colonies sent delegates to Philadelphia to form the First Continental Congress. For an entire year, the Congress tried to work out the colonists' differences with England.

By June 1776 a committee was formed to **compose** the Declaration of Independence. The committee was headed by Thomas Jefferson. After many changes to the writing of the document, a vote for its signing was taken July 4th late in the afternoon. John Hancock, President of the Continental Congress, was the first to sign the Declaration of Independence. Although the signing of the Declaration was not completed until August, the Fourth of July is the official anniversary.

Answer the following questions about "The History of the Fourth of July"
Fill in the circle next to the correct answer.

1. What is the main idea of paragraph 3?

   ○ The struggle between the United States and England
   ○ The ruling of King George
   ○ How Americans celebrate the Fourth of July
   ○ King George III sending troops to help control the fight

2. In paragraph 2, what does the word **establish** mean?

   ○ to withdraw   ○ to set up   ○ to consider   ○ to hold

3. In paragraph 3, what does the word **cry** mean?

   ○ to laugh   ○ to shout   ○ to bawl   ○ to forget

4. In paragraph 3, what does the word **unrest** mean?

   ○ to not sleep   ○ to be forceful   ○ to cover   ○ to have anxiety

5. In paragraph 4, what does the word **compose** mean?

   ○ to create   ○ to make calm   ○ to make agitated   ○ to ignore

6. What happened after the committee was formed in 1776?

   ○ John Hancock signed the Declaration of Independence
   ○ The United States went to war
   ○ The declaration of Independence was formed
   ○ King George III brings in his troops

7. What happened in the year 1941?

   ○ The Declaration of Independence was signed
   ○ John Hancock became president of the Continental Congress
   ○ Congress set the fourth of July as a legal holiday
   ○ Taxation without representation became effective

8. What was the effect of the committee that was formed in 1776?

   ○ The Declaration of Independence   ○ King George III
   ○ Thomas Jefferson heads a committee   ○ The Fourth of July

9. What does Taxation without Representation mean?

   ○ to rebel   ○ to buy without permission
   ○ to be forced to pay taxes   ○ to celebrate the Fourth of July

10. Where was the Declaration of independence signed?

    ○ Philadelphia   ○ England   ○ Texas   ○ New York

Nouns, Pronouns, and Adjectives

Underline the subject in each sentence. Write a subject pronoun that can replace it.

1. Tara and I are going to the Westside Mall tomorrow.   _____

2. Susan and Toby will be at the movie by 7:00 p.m.   _____

3. Carter and Tom are going to meet us there.   _____

4. Susan and I are hoping to see a fun new adventure.   _____

5. Tara wants to pay for the snacks.   _____

Read each sentence. Circle the adjective.

6. Mary and I are going to the miniature golf course.

7. Ed and Mark like to play miniature golf with Phil.

8. Phil goes to the putting green with Ed and Mark.

9. The girls like to play on the bumper boats with Shannon.

10. Terry also likes to ride small racing cars.

Read each sentence. Circle the common noun and underline the adjective(s).

11. The thrilling ride was finally over after three long minutes.

12. The bright red car went the fastest through the dark tunnel.

13. Cheri drove the bright yellow car to the top of the grassy hill.

14. Mary's small car was not very fast so she took the big blue bus.

15. Phil passed the three cars quickly to finish first in the race.

Identify the underlined words as a **metaphor** or a **simile**.

1. The United States was a <u>young baby of a country</u>. _____

2. The colonists were <u>as brave as lions</u>. _____

3. The war between the colonists and great Britain
   was <u>like Jack and The Bean Stalk</u>. _____

4. The battle ground <u>was an ant field of soldiers</u>. _____

5. The soldier's uniforms looked <u>like a tuxedo for a dance</u>. _____

Rewrite the paragraph in a strong voice.

      Once we gave my sister a surprise birthday party. My dad had to take her out for a quick errand so we could get the guests in the door. There were so many people at the party anxiously waiting for my sister to arrive. The door began to open and we all jumped out and yelled surprise. Little did we know it was just my grandmother arriving late to the party. Finally, we all got in our places and waited to yell surprise.

_____

_____

_____

_____

_____

_____

_____

_____

_____

Page 2
1. thick, heavy metal or weighted barrels
2. breathing and water pressure
3. around 1620
4. to sink battleships
5. It keeps the crew and equipment from being crushed by the water pressure.
6. The ballast, or weight, allows the submarine to dive. Special tanks fill with water to make the submarine heavier.
7. propellers, rudders, diving planes (steel fins), periscope, and sail
8. for months at a time

Page 3

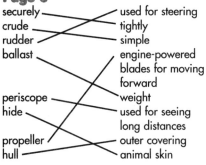

securely — tightly
crude — simple
rudder — used for steering
ballast — weight
periscope — used for seeing long distances
hide — animal skin
propeller — engine-powered blades for moving forward
hull — outer covering

Drawings will vary.

Page 5
1. largest planet in the solar system
2. hydrogen gas
3. $10\frac{1}{2}$ hours
4. 18
5. rocks, frozen gases, and ice
6. Cassini spacecraft arrived at Saturn

Page 6
1. Saturn
2. Saturn
3. Earth
4. Saturn
5. Earth
6. Earth
7. Saturn
8. Saturn
9. Saturn
10. Earth
Answers will vary.

Page 8
1. Wolves live in northern wooded areas. Their territories can be as big as 800 square miles.
2. A German shepherd dog.
3. It can have up to 20 wolves, there is a clear ranking order with strict rules, and the pack leaders are in charge.
4. Answers may vary.
   to begin their hunt and to warn outside wolves to stay away
5. Answers may vary.
   They are smart, have good eyesight, hearing and sense of smell, and work together when hunting big animals.
6. Answers may vary.
   They have a ghostly or scary sounding howl. (or) They were a threat to farmers because they could kill sheep and cattle.

Page 9
bushy and gray
75 – 120 pounds
German shepherd dog
large
42 teeth with four two-inch fangs
Alaska, Minnesota, Michigan, Wisconsin, Montana, Idaho, Washington, and Wyoming.
Live in groups, or packs, of eight to 20.
(Answers may vary)

Answers may vary.
The Three Little Pigs.
Little Red Riding Hood
and Peter and the Wolf

Page 11
1. big enough to stand in
2. in Kentucky
3. Answers may vary.
   bats, birds, raccoons, rats, and insects
4. Answers may vary.
   It is dark, cold, and damp
5. Answers may vary.
   The outer lava cools and hardens. Then the hot lava inside drains to create a cave.
6. stalactites and stalagmites
7. Answers may vary.
   deep inside caves where there is little light or wind.
8. helmet, flashlight, warm clothes, study shoes, and climbing gear

Page 12
Answers will vary.
Caves are usually dark and damp.

Caves have always been a good shelter for people.

Animals have also found shelter in caves.

Drawings will vary.

Answers will vary.

Page 13
1. S   4. S
2. C   5. C
3. S   6. C
7. My family shopped for skiing supplies, but we all didn't find what we needed.
8. My brother found the gloves he liked, and he found the suit he wanted.
9. The suit was bright red, and it had racing stripes.
10. My brother thought he might buy it, or he could use his old suit another year.

Page 14
1. RO
2. C
3. C
4. RO
5. RO
6. My friend Amanda went to every concert. Sometimes we would meet at the park and sit together.
7. Every Monday a different band would play for the eager crowd. We heard a variety of music.
8. My family really enjoyed the jazz band the best. They brought my father up on stage.
9. I will always remember the summer concerts **and** the fun we had.
10. My father said he was embarrassed to go on stage **but** he had a good time.
11. Dad likes playing the piano **or** he likes playing the saxophone.
12. These are wonderful summer memories **and** I will never forget them.

Page 15
1. S   5. P
2. S   6. P
3. P   7. S, S
4. S   8. S

1. rabbit's, dog's
2. pet store's, friend's
3. mayor's, veterinarian's
4. geese's, neighbors'
5. canaries', women's
6. girls', windows'

Page 16
1. I   8. He
2. It   9. They
3. We   10. She
4. You   11. We
5. It   12. He
6. They   13. It
7. She

Page 17

1. us	6. her
2. him	7. it
3. her	8. them
4. it	9. them
5. us	

Object pronouns for the paragraphs are: them (her class), them (the class), them (the class), him (James), her (Mrs. Smith), him (James), it (his research).

Page 18

1. I	7. I
2. me	8. I
3. I	9. me
4. I	10. me
5. I	11. I
6. I	12. I

Challenge yourself: Answers will vary.

Page 19

1. bright, radiant, warm , wet, water
2. small, shiny, new, clear
3. youngest, brand, new
4. busy, wet
5. excited, timid, water
(Answers for 6-9 will vary)
6. clear blue lake, cool crisp water
7. skillful young skier, long hot day
8. old wooden dock, long wet ride
9. small speedy boat, timid young swimmer

Adjectives for the paragraph will vary. Possible answers are: busy morning, eager family, long trip, sunny beach, big sister, yellow swimsuit, generous mother, clothing store, impatient sister, silly sister's, dresser drawers, bedroom closet, yesterday evening

Page 20

1. A	7. was thanking
2. L	8. was enjoying
3. A	9. is snapping
4. L	10. had given
5. L	11. was helping
6. L	12. have eaten

(Answers for 7-12 may vary)

Page 21

1. MV
2. HV
3. HV
4. MV
5. The librarian was putting the new books on the shelves.
6. She was listing their titles to us.
7. We were watching her stack the books.
8. Jean and I were hoping to find our favorite ones.
9. will
10. has
11. are
12. am

Page 22

1. how, when, when, where
2. how, where, when, where
3. where, when, when, how
4. where, how, where, when
5. patiently
6. inside
7. earlier
8. quickly
9. happily
10. presented yesterday, when
11. completed carefully, how
12. usually hope, when
13. listened attentively, how
14. gave in, where
Challenge yourself: answers will vary.

Page 23

1. good	8. well
2. well	9. good
3. well	10. well
4. well	11. good
5. good	12. well
6. well	13. well
7. good	14. good

Challenge yourself: answers will vary.

Page 24

Answers may vary.

1. on	7. beside
2. above	8. of
3. near	9. at
4. under	10. behind
5. in	11. on
6. near	12. by

Page 26

1. stretched out (Definitions may vary.) sentences will vary.
2. shot (Definitions may vary.) sentences will vary.
3. 3
   2
   1
   5
   4

4. anxious
5. that fireworks just don't appear in the sky.
6. "We had waited for this all year." "It seemed like the day had just started."
7. The parade extended like a snake down several city blocks.
8. Answers may vary. One possible answer is; The fire trucks were as red as cherries.
(Answers for 4-8 will vary.)

Page 28

1. The struggle between the United States and England
2. to set up
3. to shout
4. to have anxiety
5. to create
6. The declaration of Independence was formed
7. Congress set the fourth of July as a legal holiday
8. The Declaration of Independence
9. to be forced to pay taxes
10. Philadelphia

Page 29

1. Tara and I/ We
2. Susan and Toby / They
3. Carter and Tom / They
4. Susan and I/ We
5. Tara / She
6. miniature, golf
7. miniature
8. putting
9. bumper
10. small, racing
11. The thrilling ride was finally over after three long minutes
12. The bright red car went the fastest through the dark tunnel
13. Cheri drove the bright yellow car to the top of the grassy hill
14. Mary's small car was not very fast so she took the big blue bus
15. Phil passed the three cars quickly to finish first in the race

Page 30

1. metaphor
2. simile
3. simile
4. metaphor
5. simile
Rewritten paragraphs will vary.